About This Book

Welcome to the Mystery States Series

Through active participation and investigation, the Myst[...]s your students to work collaboratively while learning about each [...] is five-book series supplements and enhances your curriculum a[...], engaging way to teach your students about the U.S. regions. Each book contains a complete social studies investigation of a different region: Northeast, Southeast, Middle West, Southwest, West. Students work in cooperative groups gathering facts and information to form an investigation file to use in identifying a mystery state within each book's region. For ease of use, each book is divided into the following six sections:

- **Teacher's Guide**—Teachers are given detailed, step-by-step instructions on how to use and implement each part of the book.

- **Part 1: Discovering the Mystery State**—Students are introduced, through an original read-aloud, to a family living in the specified region. Using clues embedded in the story and provided clue cards, students work in groups to build an investigation file and identify the state in which the family lives—the mystery state.

- **Part 2: Investigating the Mystery State & Beyond**—Students investigate and research the identified mystery state by completing individual and small-group projects which involve students in a variety of social studies skills. Students also begin to learn more about other states within the region.

- **Part 3: Individual Regional Projects**—Each section contains 20 independent regional projects. These projects are designed to meet the needs of the various learning styles of students. This section also includes a contract for students to complete regarding the plans and completion dates of the selected projects. Also included is an assessment rubric for the teacher to use in evaluating the completed projects.

- **Part 4: Maps & Resources**—Each section contains related state, regional, and U.S. maps; patterns; and resource lists for literature, reference books, Web sites, and other contacts.

- **Part 5: Answer Keys & Checklist**—Each section contains a detailed answer key as well as a reproducible checklist that a teacher can use to keep track of each activity completed by each student.

Benefits of the Mystery States Series:
- Supports national social studies standards developed by the National Council for the Social Studies (NCSS)
- Supplements and enhances fourth- and fifth-grade social studies curricula
- Contains a step-by-step teacher's guide
- Encourages active involvement through independent and small-group activities
- Requires higher-order thinking skills and targets different learning styles
- Promotes students' success

Teacher's Guide

Part 1: Discovering the Mystery State

Part 1 is designed to be completed in the step-by-step order presented below. In this section, students are introduced to a family living in a mystery state within the Southwest region through a read-aloud story. Students work in small groups to uncover clues embedded in the story as well as complete other activities in which they work in collaborative groups researching, interpreting, and analyzing information to help them predict the mystery state's identity.

Step 1: Have four different students, in turn, locate one of these states on a U.S. wall map: Arizona, New Mexico, Oklahoma, and Texas. Inform your students that they've just identified the states of the Southwest region.

Step 2: Divide students into six groups. Give each group a copy of "Lace and Curls" (pages 8–14). Also, give each student one copy of "Investigation File" (page 15), "Investigation State Checklist" (page 17), the regional and U. S. maps (pages 39 and 40), and a file folder. (Have students keep all reproducibles and gathered research in the file folder throughout the investigation.) Instruct the students in each group to label each Southwest state on their regional maps (page 39). Then direct the students to use a red crayon or colored pencil to shade in the Southwest region on their U.S. maps (page 40).

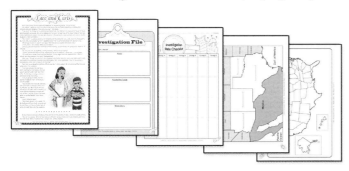

Step 3: Tell students that they are about to become supersleuths in an investigation of the Southwest region. Explain that you're going to read aloud a story about a family who lives in a state within the Southwest region. Direct students to listen carefully as you read the story. Next, tell your students that you're going to read the story a second time, but this time each student is to jot down on the "Notes" section of her "Investigation File" (page 15) any clues that the story reveals about the state in which the family lives. Remind students to listen for clues, such as geographic references, climate/weather information, and references to occupations, food, plants, and/or animals.

Step 4: After reading the story, allow time for students to compare notes within their groups. Then have a representative from each group read aloud the clues her group discovered. Encourage each group to add to its notes any clues not listed. Have each group evaluate the revised clues and then list in the "Possibilities/Leads" section of page 15 any states in which they think Jimmy's family might live.

Step 5: Make a copy of page 16; then cut the reproducible into six separate clue cards. Distribute one clue card to each group and inform the group it has several clues to research that will help bring the class closer to the mystery state's identity. Provide ample time for each group to research its clues. Make available a variety of regional references as well as almanacs, encyclopedias, and atlases. (For a list of resources, see page 42.)

Step 6: Hold a conference with each group once it has answered its clues. If the answers are incorrect, guide the group toward finding the correct answers.

Step 7: Have a member of each group read aloud her group's clues and answers. Instruct each student to record each group's clues and answers on the back of her "Investigation File" for future reference.

Step 8: Have each group use the "Investigation State Checklist" (page 17) to check off any states that could possibly be Jimmy's home based on the gathered clues and clue card information. Then have each group read aloud the states it checked as the other groups record the information in the appropriate columns on their checklists.

Step 9: Instruct each group to use the checklist to eliminate any states not considered as the mystery state and record those states at the bottom of page 15. Then have the group use the checklist information to help it predict the mystery state's identity. After coming to a consensus, have each group member write her prediction on the back of the checklist.

Step 10: Give each student one copy of "Crack the Code" (page 18). Have the student find out the mystery state's identity by completing the reproducible as directed. Take a poll to see how many groups made correct predictions.

The five activities in this section are designed to be completed in any order. Also, the activities are independent of one another so you can select the activities that best fit your students' needs. Each activity can be completed individually, in pairs, or in small groups.

News About New Mexico (Pages 20–22)
(Research, Writing)

By completing this activity, students will become more familiar with the mystery state—New Mexico. Students are challenged to research topics related to New Mexico, such as location, land features, natural resources, climate and weather, Native Americans, and more.

Materials for each student or group of students: 1 copy each of pages 20, 21, and 22; access to references on New Mexico and the Southwest region

Directions: Make available various resources on New Mexico and the Southwest region (see resource list on page 42). After students research the various topics and take notes, have them write complete sentences about each topic in the appropriate sections of pages 20, 21, and 22. If desired, gather the completed work and staple each set of reproducibles along the top, creating a flip booklet. Post each booklet on a bulletin board titled "News About New Mexico." Enlarge, cut out, and color the New Mexico symbols on page 41 and post them around the display. As an extension activity, have students work in pairs or small groups to research the three other Southwest states, using the same topics listed on pages 20 through 22. This will provide excellent information students can use to compare the four Southwest states.

Balloons Over Albuquerque (Pages 23–24)
(Research, Writing)

This activity will help students research the Albuquerque International Balloon Fiesta and learn more about hot-air balloons.

Materials for each student: 1 copy of pages 23 and 24; various reference materials on Albuquerque, New Mexico, and hot-air balloons; pencil; crayons or markers; file folder

Directions: Direct students to use the reference materials to help them complete page 23 on another sheet of paper. Then have students use their research from page 23 to help them write a newspaper article and add a picture in the space provided on page 24. Instruct the students to display page 23, their research, and page 24 in a file folder as shown. Finally, direct the students to title the front of their folders "Balloons Over Albuquerque" and decorate them.

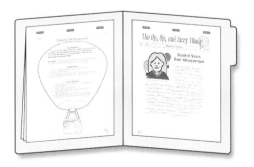
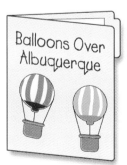

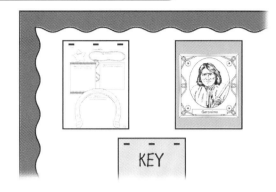

Guess Who (Pages 25–27)
(Researching a Notable Person, Writing)

This activity will allow students to research notable persons from New Mexico, such as actors, writers, and scientists.

Materials for each student or group of students: 1 copy of page 25, 1 enlarged illustration from page 26 or 27, one 9" x 12" sheet of colored construction paper, glue

Directions: In advance, make two or three enlarged copies of each illustration on pages 26 and 27. (Enlargements should be no bigger than 8¹/₂" x 11".) Next, assign each student or group of students one of the notable persons from pages 26 and 27. Supply each student or group with the materials listed. Then direct students to complete page 25 by using encyclopedias and various other reference materials. Inform students not to use the person's name anywhere on the front of page 25. Once students complete page 25, assign each student or group of students a number to write in the space provided on page 25. Next, have them glue the enlarged illustrations onto the colored construction paper. Display students' work on a bulletin board titled "Who's Who Gallery." Randomly mount the "Guess Who" pages, the illustrations, and a key (covered with a sheet of construction paper that is stapled along the top edge) as shown. Encourage students to visit the board, read the "Guess Who" pages, and guess the identities of the notable people by writing their names on a sheet of lined paper. Once students have guessed each person's identity, direct them to check their guesses by lifting up the construction paper cover and looking at the key.

Investigating Bats (Pages 28–30)
(Research, Writing)

In this activity, students will research the bats living in Carlsbad Caverns National Park in New Mexico. Then they will conduct a survey to determine people's attitudes about bats.

Materials for each student or group of students: 1 copy each of pages 28, 29, and 30; access to various reference materials on bats, Carlsbad Caverns National Park, and New Mexico; poster board; markers or crayons

Directions:

Step 1: Have each student or group research bats using the information on page 28; then have them use their research to complete the survey on page 29. Direct students to write "true" or "false" next to each survey question on page 29. Then challenge the student to ask three people the survey questions. Have the student record each person's response in the space provided on the survey sheet.

Step 2: After students complete page 29, have them use the survey to help them sketch a poster highlighting some of the misconceptions people have about bats in the space provided on page 30. Then have each student create a poster promoting bat awareness and Carlsbad Caverns. Display the posters around your room and discuss the results of each student's survey.

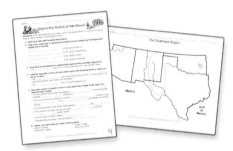

Beyond the Borders of New Mexico (Pages 31–32)
(Mapmaking, Research)

This mapmaking activity takes students beyond the borders of New Mexico to learn more about the three other states in the Southwest region.

Materials for each student or group of students: 1 copy of page 31, 1 enlarged copy of page 32 on an 11" x 14" sheet of paper, crayons or colored pencils

Directions: Provide each student or group of students with the materials listed. Also make available various reference materials on the Southwest region (see resource list on page 42). Instruct each student or group of students to complete pages 31 and 32 as directed. If desired, place an enlarged outline map of the Southwest region (see map on page 39) labeled with the appropriate state names in the center of a bulletin board. Arrange the student-created maps around the enlarged map. Title the display "Beyond the Borders of New Mexico."

Part 3: Individual Regional Projects

The research topics, contracts, and rubric in this section are designed to provide each student with an opportunity to successfully complete research on the Southwest region. The projects are grouped into four quadrants according to different learning styles.

Pick-a-Project (Pages 34–36)
(Research)

Materials for each student: 1 copy each of pages 34, 35, and 36; access to various reference materials on the Southwest region; a variety of art supplies

Directions:

Step 1: Assign each student (or allow them to choose) one or more projects from one or more quadrants on page 34.

Step 2: Provide each student with a copy of the "Pick-a-Project Contract" (page 35). After discussing due dates and other pertinent information, direct each student to complete the contract(s) and sign at the bottom. After reviewing each student's contract, add your signature at the bottom.

Step 3: Provide each student with a copy of the "Pick-a-Project Rubric" (page 36). Discuss the grading criteria on the rubric with your students. After a student completes each assigned project, use the rubric to evaluate her project. (Page 36 can be used to evaluate up to four projects per student.) Using the rubric will help you evaluate each student's project(s) on eight different criteria, using a scale of 1 to 5 (1 = Poor, 3 = Good, 5 = Outstanding).

Part 4: Maps & Resources

Part 4 contains related state, regional, and U.S. maps; symbols; and resource lists for related literature and reference books, Web sites, and other contacts. Many of the maps and resources are used in conjunction with the activities in Part 1 and Part 2.

- New Mexico Outline Map (page 38)
- The Southwestern States (page 39)
- The United States (page 40)
- Symbols of New Mexico (page 41)
- Resource Guide (page 42)

Part 5: Answer Keys & Checklist

Part 5 contains a detailed answer key as well as a reproducible checklist that you can use to keep track of each activity completed by each student.

PART 1: DISCOVERING THE MYSTERY STATE

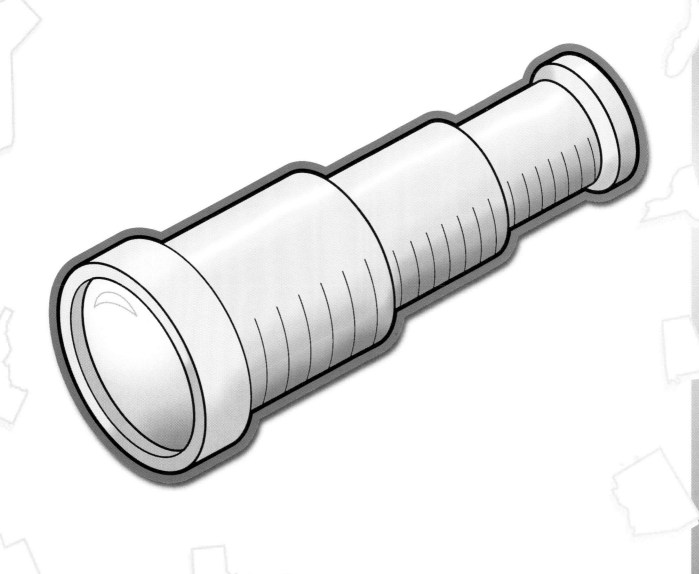

Jimmy flung open the front door and called out his standard greeting, "I'm not home!"

"Me, either!" replied his mom from the kitchen where she was busily preparing something that smelled zesty and delightful. "How was your day?" she asked.

"The usual," he droned as he routinely sauntered down the hallway to his bedroom to dump his backpack filled with homework. But as he stepped into his room, he saw none of his usual clutter. In fact, set on his nightstand in place of his usual pile of papers, chewed pencils, and assorted coins was a colorful bouquet of fresh cut flowers.

"Am I home?" he asked himself as he headed out to the kitchen to see if that voice truly belonged to his mom. Mrs. Davis looked up from a bubbling pot of chili to see her perplexed son staring at her.

"What happened to my room?" he began. "And why are you cooking dinner so early?"

"Think, honey," she smiled. "What day is it today?"

Jimmy's expressionless face mirrored his blank memory, so she hinted, "I'm going to the airport in 15 minutes."

"No one ever tells me anything," Jimmy declared. "Where are you going?"

"To pick up Barb and Kara, who are staying with us for the weekend. Remember?" she prodded.

"Oh, yeah, your college friend and her daughter," Jimmy began and then stopped short. "Wait a minute, are they staying in my room?" he demanded.

"Well, yes, I thought you wouldn't mind sleeping in the family room. It's just for two nights and I really want Barb and Kara to feel welcome and comfortable," Mrs. Davis responded. "Hey, it's not so bad; I cleaned your entire room. It took me all morning!"

"But I don't even know this girl Kara. What's she like?" Jimmy asked, still not convinced that this was going to be a fun weekend.

"I've never actually met her, but if she's anything like her mother, she'll be easy to get along with. Barb and I hit it off on the first day of college and have remained friends ever since."

"Are you going to saddle me with having to entertain her?" Jimmy questioned candidly.

"You certainly don't have to, but Kara has never been to this part of the country. Wouldn't you like to show her how spectacular Paradise Hills is? Maybe you could take her exploring or maybe we can all take a day trip to one of the state parks to see the deserts!" Mrs. Davis offered.

Jimmy rolled his eyes.

"Well, think about it," she added. "I'll be back around five o'clock; once we get to know Kara we'll have a better idea of what she might like to do this weekend."

• • • • • • • • • • • • • • •

At the sound of car doors shutting, Jimmy glanced out the window to steal a preliminary peek at Kara.

"Oh, no!" he gasped. "She's all lace and curls. All she's going to want to do is go shopping and have her nails done. What a weekend this is going to be," Jimmy moaned.

He retreated to the bathroom where he figured he'd be safe for a few minutes. He heard the front door open and then recognized one of the two voices that was engaged in excited chatter. After several minutes his mom called out, "Jimmy, we're home. Come meet Barb and Kara, honey."

Jimmy flushed the toilet; ran the water in the sink, pretending to wash his hands; took a deep breath; and then opened the door, whispering, "Here goes nothing!"

He ambled directly over to his mom, who proudly put her arm around him and stated, "Barb and Kara, this is my son, Jimmy, whom I've been telling you about. He's very excited about showing you around. Aren't you, honey?"

Jimmy forced a polite smile and managed to say, "Yeah, sure…it's nice to meet you."

Barb came right up to him, hugged him, and said, "I feel like I know you already. But you're even more handsome than your mother said. Isn't he, Kara?" Both Kara and Jimmy turned crimson at that comment, and there was an awkward pause until Mrs. Davis came to the rescue.

"Oh, where are my manners? You must be starving. Jimmy, please get their bags from the car and take them down to their room. I'm sure our tired travelers would like to freshen up before dinner. I'll step into the kitchen and put the finishing touches on our meal. Dad should be home in about 15 minutes. Then we can all sit down together."

Dinner was exceptional. Everything was spicy and plentiful except for the conversation between Jimmy and Kara. Every time Jimmy asked a question, all he got in reply was a nod or a quiet "no." By the end of the evening all he had learned about this girl who was going to be invading his space was that she dressed quite girlishly, was painfully shy, and was unbelievably quiet.

● ● ● ● ● ● ● ● ● ● ● ● ● ● ●

Things were going from bad to worse. Jimmy spent a horrible night sleeping in the family room. There were howls and moans in this part of the house that he wasn't used to, and even though he wasn't scared, he kept waking up throughout the night. He finally gave up trying to get a good night's sleep and stumbled into the kitchen to get a glass of orange juice.

"What am I going to do with her today?" he wondered. But Jimmy didn't have long to wonder. His mom led Barb and Kara into the kitchen for breakfast and announced that they were going shopping.

"I can't wait to see all the exquisite turquoise jewelry," swooned Barb. "Kara and I are going to shop till we drop!" she giggled.

After a quick and quiet breakfast, the ladies bustled about, readying themselves for their shopping adventure.

"Are you sure you won't join us?" Barb asked Jimmy as they headed for the front door.

"Oh, I'm positive!" he assured her. "I'll find something to do. Dad can always use an extra hand around the ranch."

Jimmy pumped his arm to celebrate this incredible stroke of good luck when Kara pulled her mother aside and whispered something in her ear. Barb looked very concerned and then retreated with her daughter to their bedroom. Several minutes later Barb returned to explain that Kara was feeling very nauseous and wasn't up to going shopping.

"She's got to be sick to turn down the chance to go shopping. Frankly, I'm a bit worried," Barb said.

"Could it be the change in food?" Mrs. Davis asked. "I find that when I travel and eat food from another part of the country my stomach doesn't always agree with my choices."

"Maybe," Barb said. "Oh, I'm so disappointed." She paused and then said, "Well, tomorrow's another day. Perhaps we can go shopping then."

"Oh, don't be silly," Mrs. Davis countered. "Kara simply needs to rest and let her stomach settle. Jimmy will be here if she needs anything and Dan is out on the ranch where Jimmy can reach him at any time. There's nothing to worry about. We can even call to check in with Jimmy every hour or so, if you'd like."

"Well, let me just run it by Kara," Barb said as she turned to walk down the hall. She was back within seconds.

"She's sound asleep," Barb reported. "I guess the flight and all have really taken their toll on her."

"Oh, the poor thing," Mrs. Davis added. "Let's go and bring back something special for her. Jimmy, you don't mind hanging around the house in case Kara wakes up and needs something, do you?"

"No," Jimmy answered. "I'll be a good baby-sitter!" he added with a laugh.

● ● ● ● ● ● ● ● ● ● ● ● ● ●

Several hours passed smoothly as Jimmy read his latest issue of *National Geographic Adventure,* helped himself to a snack, and watched sports on TV for a while. He was just flipping through the channels when he heard Kara say, "Where is everyone?"

"I'm right here!" he replied.

Kara smiled but glanced around the room as she said, "No, really, where did our moms go?"

"They went shopping. Your mom didn't want to wake you up," he replied. "Hey, how are you feeling?"

"Fine," she answered. "But I am disappointed. I really wanted to see some native turquoise."

"Well, I could show you *real* native turquoise—not set in jewelry but right in its natural state," he suggested.

"What do you mean?" Kara asked.

"I found turquoise about half a mile from here," he said.

"Are you serious?" Kara said, her face brightening with excitement.

"Yeah. Are you up for a walk?" he asked.

"If we're going to find turquoise, absolutely!" Kara declared.

Ten minutes later, after leaving a note for his dad, Jimmy led Kara outside. The sun was directly overhead and Jimmy was concerned that Kara might not be used to this type of climate.

"Are you sure you're feeling up to this?" he asked her.

"Yep, I'm fine," Kara said.

They walked along in silence for a while, Jimmy feeling a little awkward, and not knowing what to talk about. Usually he had no trouble talking to girls, but the girls he knew were cool. They were quite talkative, but Kara was so quiet. At first this irritated him, but as they walked on in silence, Jimmy began to feel challenged to break Kara out of her shell. He wanted to entertain her, make her laugh, and have her enjoy herself for once in her quiet little life. He looked up ahead and saw a sign that warned of unstable ground. He smiled to himself as he hatched a plan.

"Um, Kara, see that sign?" he asked as he pointed up ahead. "Be really careful not to get too close to it. There's a sinkhole in that area and if you step on that spot, you'll fall down into the earth."

He had captured her attention. "What do you mean? What's a sinkhole?" she asked, full of wide-eyed wonder.

"Oh, it's like an express elevator ride straight down into a cave…without the elevator," he laughed. "It's actually formed when part of a cave's ceiling collapses and makes a new entrance into the cave."

"Is it safe to enter a cave through a sinkhole?" Kara asked.

"No!" he exclaimed. "There's no telling how far down the bottom of the cave is. Then, even if you live through the fall, you can't climb your way back out because usually the walls are angled too steeply or they're too wet and slippery."

It seemed like Jimmy had found a subject that Kara was interested in. She earnestly continued with more questions.

"So there must be a cave around here. Have you ever been inside it?" she pressed on.

"Yeah, there's a safe entrance on the other side of this hill," he answered as he walked dangerously close to the sinkhole warning sign. "Maybe we can check it out later. First, we'll have to go home to change our clothes and get some gear. You should never go cave exploring without flashlights and rope," he added.

"Jimmy, watch out," Kara warned. "You're getting too close to that sign."

Jimmy smiled to himself—his plan was working. Kara was animated and alive! He turned his back to the sign, faced Kara, and continued to walk backward.

"Kara, I was just wondering, do you like bats? Caves around here are homes to bats and we might get to see some when we go inside the cave later on," he said.

As he was studying Kara's face to see her reaction to this new piece of information, he misjudged exactly how close he truly was to the hole. Suddenly, he felt his right foot sink as if in quicksand, but before he could react to yank it out, the ground around him gave way and he was falling down into the depths below.

Kara screamed, "Jimmy!" and ran toward the sinkhole as close as she dared to go. But, fearing the same fate, she wisely decided to keep back a few steps. She called his name several more times and prayed she'd hear a reply, but all she heard were the echoes of falling rocks hitting the ground far below.

After the initial shock, Kara sprang into action. Jimmy needed her; she had to find the other entrance to the cave. But she knew she shouldn't enter any pitch-black, chilly cavern dressed the way she was. She turned to head back to the house for supplies and frantically scanned the landscape for familiar markings. Luckily, it was a pretty direct route, and after running for about 15 minutes, she spotted the ranch up ahead. By the time she burst through the front door she had a plan. She ran into Jimmy's room and searched for pants, sweatshirts, and socks. She grabbed two sets of each; then she scribbled a hasty note and left it on the kitchen counter. Next, she rushed into the garage to hunt for a flashlight and some rope. She found some rope hanging right above a bike and she decided to take the bike, too, to cut down on time. She stuffed her supplies and clothes into a backpack she spotted and then took off.

Riding the bike shaved several minutes off her return trip, but it still seemed to take forever. Kara rode to the site where she had last seen Jimmy in hopes that he would be there now. When he wasn't, she continued on in the direction that she thought would bring her to the cave's entrance. As she circled around to the other side of the hill, she felt a cool puff of air blowing toward her. She followed the breeze and was led right to the mouth of the cave. Her entire body felt jittery. As she dismounted the bike, her legs had the strength of overcooked noodles. Thinking about Jimmy being trapped in the cave with a strong possibility of being injured helped her rise above her fears. She searched through the backpack and pulled out a set of clothes, slipped them on, and then took a glance around at the outside world. She spotted a solid-looking stick and, thinking that it might make a good walking stick, picked it up. With the flashlight clutched in her other hand and the backpack on her back, she took a deep breath and stepped inside the cave. She counted five steps and then stopped to get a sense of her surroundings. Using her flashlight as her eyes, she looked all around and marveled at what she saw. There were glistening stalactites shooting down from the ceiling and earthy brown stalagmites rising out of the ground. All the walls were moist and when the beam of light struck them, they looked like sheets of sparkling diamonds. Just out of curiosity, she flicked off the light for a second and was overwhelmed with the total blackness—she held her hand directly in front of her face and couldn't even see it. An eerie silence began to affect her; it was so profoundly quiet that the pounding of her own heartbeat seemed to be echoing off the walls. She decided to call out to Jimmy with the hope that her voice would shatter the silence he was enveloped in. She called, "Jim—my, Jim—my, where are you?" and waited. A second time she yelled, "Jim-my, Jim-my, can you hear me?" but again heard nothing except the echo of her own voice. She picked up on a faint squeaking sound that soon rose to a crescendo of squeals as a thick clump of thrashing bats came darting furiously toward her. She immediately dropped to her knees, and, in an effort to cover her head with her hands, she lost her grip on her flashlight and it rolled out of reach. Fortunately, the light stayed on and after the bats vanished, Kara crawled over to retrieve it. The ground was quite muddy and cold, and in spite of the warm clothes she had on, Kara noticed her teeth were chattering. She stood up, resolving to find Jimmy quickly since she realized how cold he must be. Using her walking stick as a guide, she took small firm steps along the straight path, stopping every few minutes to call out Jimmy's name. She continued, ducking now and again to avoid long stalactites that jutted down at her. Wondering how much farther she might have to go, she shone the light up ahead and panicked when she saw the path lead up to a crevice. She rushed up to it and pushed her walking stick through, but that was all that could fit into the space. She shone her light into the slit but couldn't see beyond several feet on the other side. Had she hit a dead end? She hadn't seen any other paths off this one, so how was she ever going to find Jimmy now? "Oh, no!" she sighed in exasperation as she plunked down on the muddy floor to gather her thoughts.

After weighing her various options, Kara decided to retreat and get help. Thinking about how much time she had wasted already and about how cold and possibly hurt Jimmy was right now, she felt so guilty that she had tried to handle this on her own. She really should have called for help when she was back at the ranch, but she wanted to prove to everyone, including herself, that she was more than a quiet, demure little girl who lived solely to shop and look good.

She stood up to go when she thought she heard something. She stopped to listen…. There it was again. It sounded like someone calling out. Yes, it really was! But where was it coming from? She listened intently again and heard, "Hey, is anyone there?" It seemed to be coming from the crack in the wall.

Kara screamed as loudly as she could through the crevice, "Jimmy, it's Kara! Are you hurt?"

"Kara? Really?" Jimmy sounded shocked.

"Yes, are you okay?" she asked again.

"My leg's broken and I'm freezing," he answered. "Do you have any rope with you?"

"Yeah, why?" Kara asked.

"Do you see any water over there?" he asked.

Kara shone her light at the muddy ground and saw what looked like a deep stream that went under the wall.

"I see it; does it go near you, too?" she asked.

"Yes, and I think I can swim under it. Hold one end of the rope and send the rest under to me," he replied.

"Wait," she called out. She lowered her walking stick into the stream to see how deep the water was. It never touched the bottom so the water was at least four feet deep.

"Okay, here it comes," Kara called out as she unwound the coiled rope and clutched onto her end.

A minute later Jimmy yelled, "I've got it. Now hold on tightly. I'm going to lower myself into the water and try to follow the rope to you."

Kara was so worried. She kept shining her light into the water to illuminate the area for him. She could feel Jimmy tugging on the rope and tightened her grip even more. Finally, after what seemed an eternity, Jimmy surfaced on her side. She dropped to her knees and reached for him, then grabbed him under his arms and helped haul him out of the water.

"I'm so glad to see you," she exclaimed as she fished through the backpack and pulled out his warm clothes. "Here, take off your wet shirt and put this warm sweatshirt on," she instructed.

Jimmy did as he was told and even let Kara help him. He was obviously in a lot of pain and resigned to letting someone else take over. She looked at his leg and could tell that the break was right below the knee. She tied a supportive splint for him by ripping his wet shirt into strips and using them to tie her stick alongside his leg.

"Does anything else hurt right now?" she asked.

"Some other scrapes and cuts, but they're not so bad. Hey, we've got to get out of here—how are we going to do that?" he asked.

"I'll help you up, and then you'll have to lean on me," she started. "Put all your weight on your good leg and on me and we'll just take one step at a time," she advised.

So with the flashlight in her left hand and Jimmy leaning heavily on her right side, Kara guided them slowly through the cave. They moved on in silence. This time it wasn't a lack of knowing what to say, but an effort to channel their energy into the rescue. As they approached the cave's entrance, Kara thought she heard voices. Shielding her eyes from the blinding sunlight, she stepped out to see quite a gathering of people.

After finding Kara's note, her mother and Mr. and Mrs. Davis had assembled an entire rescue team that was readying to enter the cave.

"There they are, thank God!" shrieked Kara's mother. Four EMTs rushed up to Kara and Jimmy—two laid Jimmy on a stretcher and two offered one to Kara.

"Oh, no thanks, I'm fine," Kara replied politely.

"Please, miss, you probably feel better than you look, but we need to be sure," a concerned man said.

Kara thought that was a strange comment until she looked at herself. She was literally covered with mud and scrapes and her fingers were a pale blue. She sat down on the stretcher and for the first time realized how exhausted she was. She turned to see how Jimmy was and saw that he was staring at her.

"Kara, I'm really sorry," he whispered.

"For what, giving me the adventure of a lifetime?!" Kara said.

"No, for misjudging you," he replied. "Nothing but lace and curls? *No way!*"

Investigation File

Investigator's Name: _____

Notes

Possibilities/Leads

Eliminations

15

Clue Cards

CLUE #1

Jimmy lives in a town called Paradise Hills.

1. Which states west of 95°W longitude and north of 30°N latitude have a city or town with Paradise in its name?
2. Which of these states are located in the Southwest region?

CLUE #2

In the state where Jimmy lives there are large reserves of petroleum.

1. Which states west of 95°W longitude and north of 30°N latitude mine petroleum?
2. Which of these states are located in the Southwest region?

CLUE #3

Jimmy's mother suggests that they go on a day trip to one of the state parks to see the deserts.

1. Which states have deserts?
2. Which of these states are located in the Southwest region?

CLUE #4

Jimmy lives on a ranch where his dad works.

1. Which states west of 95°W longitude and north of 30°N latitude have cattle ranches?
2. Which of these states are located in the Southwest region?

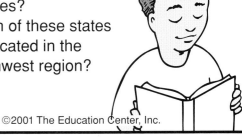

CLUE #5

Jimmy tells Kara that they can find turquoise.

1. In what states is turquoise found?
2. Which of these states are located in the Southwest region?

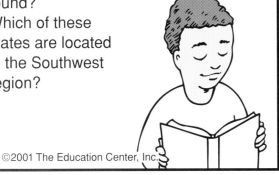

CLUE #6

In the state where Jimmy lives the largest city has over 350,000 people.

1. Which states west of 95°W longitude and north of 30°N latitude have capital cities with at least 350,000 people?
2. Which of these states are located in the Southwest region?

Investigation State Checklist

STATES	Group 1	Group 2	Group 3	Group 4	Group 5	Group 6
Arizona						
New Mexico						
Oklahoma						
Texas						

Crack the Code

Directions: To discover the nickname and name of the mystery state, use the code below to help you write a letter from the grid that matches each ordered pair of symbols. Write the corresponding letter in the blank above each symbol.

Example: (■ ●) = K

▲	A	F	P	U	R
●	Q	G	L	K	J
+	C	H	M	B	W
■	D	I	N	S	X
◆	E	V	O	T	Y/Z

▲ ● + ■ ◆

N E W — M E X I C O — I S
(+■) (▲◆) (◆+) (++) (▲◆) (◆■) (●■) (▲+) (+◆) (●■) (■■)

T H E — L A N D — O F
(■◆) (●+) (▲◆) (+●) (▲▲) (+■) (▲■) (+◆) (●▲)

E N C H A N T M E N T.
(▲◆) (+■) (▲+) (●+) (▲▲) (+■) (■◆) (++) (▲◆) (+■) (■◆)

PART 2:
INVESTIGATING
THE MYSTERY STATE
& BEYOND

Name(s) _____

20

News About New Mexico

Physical Land Features

State Capital: _____

State Tree: _____

State Flower: _____

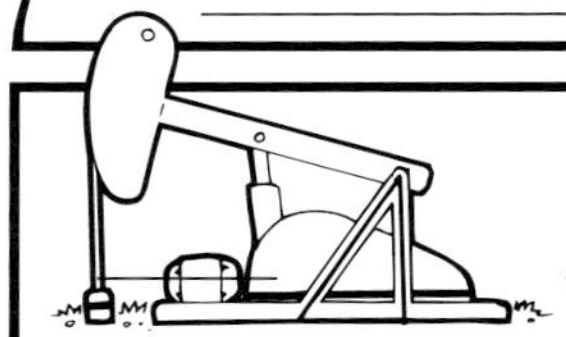

State Bird: _____

Natural Resources

Location

N
E
W
S

Climate & Weather

Name(s) _____

Famous Landmarks

History

Native Americans

Food

Famous People

21

Name(s) _____

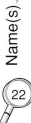

Plants

Places of Interest

Economy

Animals

Balloons Over Albuquerque

Congratulations!
The Up, Up, and Away Times has chosen you as the winner
of a ride in a hot-air balloon over the city of Albuquerque.
The *Times* will publish a front-page article, written by you,
describing this fantastic flight.

Directions: To ensure that you write the best possible article, research
the questions below on Albuquerque and hot-air balloons.

Albuquerque

1. What is the Albuquerque International Balloon Fiesta?
2. When is the fiesta held?
3. How long does the fiesta last? How many balloonists participate?
4. Why is Albuquerque a great spot for a balloon festival?

Hot-Air Balloons

1. What are the two main parts of a hot-air balloon and
   what do they do?
2. How do hot-air balloons rise?
3. During what times of day do most hot-air balloon
   flights take place?
4. Who was the first person to fly in a hot-air balloon?
5. What is the longest recorded hot-air balloon flight?

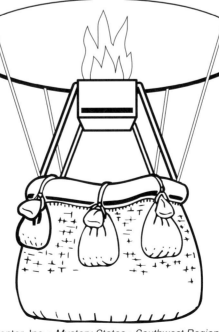

The Up, Up, and Away Times

Vol. 1 No. 1   **Weekend Edition** $1.00

Student Soars Over Albuquerque

by

_____

_____

_____

_____

_____

_____

Student takes to the air this week.

_____

_____

_____

_____

_____

_____

_____

_____

_____

_____

_____

_____

_____

Guess Who

Number
_____

Clue 1: Birthdate

_____

Clue 2: Occupation/profession for which this person is most noted

_____
_____
_____
_____
_____
_____
_____

Clue 3: Information that ties this person to the state of New Mexico

_____
_____
_____
_____
_____
_____

Clue 4: More specific details about this person and his/her accomplishments

_____
_____
_____
_____
_____
_____

Who's Who Gallery

John Denver

Bill Mauldin

Kit Carson

Nancy Lopez

Judy Blume

Conrad Nicholson Hilton

Who's Who Gallery

Geronimo

Willa Sibert Cather

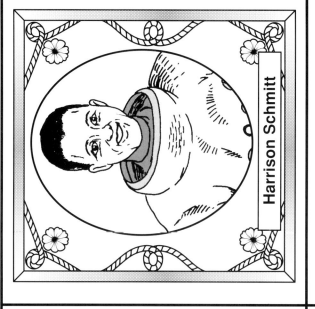

Harrison Schmitt

Robert Oppenheimer

Georgia O'Keeffe

Billy the Kid

Dear Students,

The New Mexico department of tourism is seeking help from all students regarding a serious threat to our tourist industry. As you know, Carlsbad Caverns is a favorite New Mexico tourist attraction. In the past few months there has been a decrease in the number of tourists visiting the caverns. We believe it has something to do with people's fears of the Mexican freetail bats that live there. We would like you to conduct research on bats and people's attitudes toward them. Below you will find a list of topics that we would like you to research. It is important that we find a way to better educate the public about bats. We appreciate your help.

Sincerely,

Bert Andrew Thomas
Tourism Committee

- Are bats birds?
- Can other mammals fly?
- Are bats blind?
- How many bat species live in the United States?
- Do bats attack people?
- Do bats have many babies at once?
- Do most bats feed on the blood of other animals?
- Do bats live in other places besides caves?
- Do bats navigate with their ears?
- Are bats good for the environment?

Name _____

Bat Awareness Survey

Survey Questions	True/False Answer	True/False Response		
		Name _____	Name _____	Name _____
Bats are birds.				
Bats are the only mammals that can fly.				
Bats are blind.				
Forty species of bats live in the United States.				
Bats attack people.				
Most female bats only have one baby at a time.				
Most bats feed on the blood of other animals.				
Bats only live in caves.				
Some bats use their ears to navigate.				
Bats damage the environment.				
This person has accurate knowledge about bats.				

Name _____

Get Better Informed About Bats

Continue helping the New Mexico tourism department make people better informed about the bats that live in Carlsbad Caverns by creating a poster that highlights some of this unique mammal's characteristics. Use your research and completed survey form (pages 28 and 29) to help you sketch a draft of your poster in the space provided below.

Name _____

 **Beyond the Borders of New Mexico**

Directions: Follow the directions in the order in which they appear below to complete the map on page 32. Write answers on the blanks provided.

1. **Label each state with its postal abbreviation.**

2. **Draw a star on the map to represent the location of each capital city. Then label each capital city on the map.**

    • _____ is the capital of Arizona.

    • _____ is the capital of New Mexico.

    • _____ is the capital of Texas.

    • _____ is the capital of Oklahoma.

3. **Draw three brown triangles to represent the location of the mountain range below.**
    The _____ stretch from northern New Mexico through western Texas.

4. **Label the map with a red box to show where each of the following desert or canyon areas are located.**
    • The _____ was formed by the Colorado River. It lies along the Colorado River between Lake Powell and Lake Mead.
    • The _____ lies across southwest Arizona.

5. **Use a blue crayon or marker to color or trace each body of water on the map. Then label the body of water.**
    • The Rio Grande flows through the middle of _____. It forms the border between _____ and Mexico.

    • The source of the Pecos River is in northern _____. It flows through _____ and _____ and empties into the Rio Grande.

    • The Red River forms most of the border between _____ and _____.

    • The Colorado River flows through northwest _____ and forms _____ western border.

    • Eufaula Lake is located in eastern _____.

    • Galveston Bay is located on the east coast of _____.

6. **Lightly color each state according to the key below.**
    Arizona—yellow   Texas—orange
    New Mexico—green   Oklahoma—pink

The Southwest Region

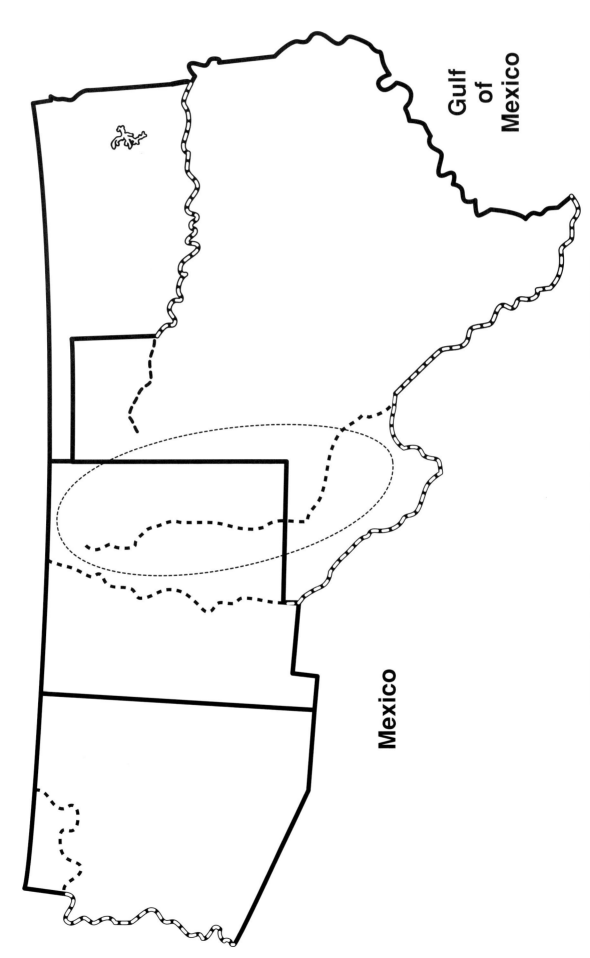

Gulf
of
Mexico

Mexico

PART 3: INDIVIDUAL REGIONAL PROJECTS

Pick-a-Project

Group 1

- ☐ Make a poster highlighting ten little-known facts about the Southwest.

- ☐ List 15 places you would like to visit in the Southwest.

- ☐ Make a timeline showing important events in New Mexico's history.

- ☐ Make a weeklong itinerary for a person visiting New Mexico.

- ☐ Make a recipe box with five recipes from the Southwest.

Group 2

- ☐ Write a paragraph comparing a state in the Southwest to the state you live in.

- ☐ Write four journal entries from Kara's point of view: two entries before the accident and two entries after the accident.

- ☐ Write a poem about a famous tourist site in the Southwest.

- ☐ Give an oral report about a famous historical figure from New Mexico.

- ☐ Write an editorial for a newspaper explaining advantages and disadvantages of living in the Southwest.

Group 3

- ☐ Write a how-to paragraph about cave exploring.

- ☐ Write five questions you would like to ask a person living in the Southwest.

- ☐ Summarize the important events in Southwest history.

- ☐ Design an advertisement for a product grown in the Southwest.

- ☐ Compare and contrast the Southwest with the Southeast.

Group 4

- ☐ Pretend you work for a newspaper. Write an article about traveling across the Southwest.

- ☐ Choose a scene from "Lace and Curls" to dramatize for the class.

- ☐ Draw a map of the Southwest and add places you would like to visit on vacation.

- ☐ Write a song about one of the states in the Southwest.

- ☐ Design a postcard from a state in the Southwest.

Pick-a-Project Contract

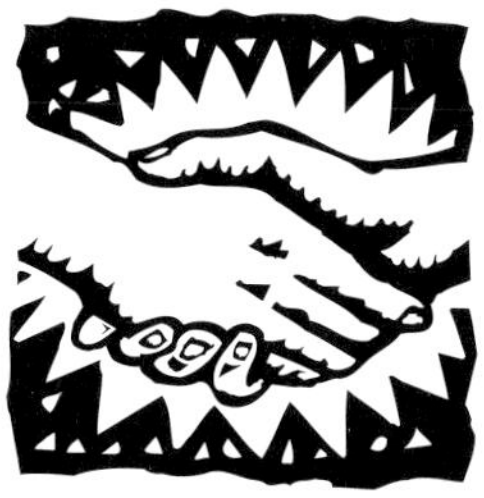

Name _____

Project _____

Due date _____

Materials/resources needed _____

_____

Plan for completing project _____

_____

_____

_____

Student signature _____ Teacher signature _____

Pick-a-Project Contract

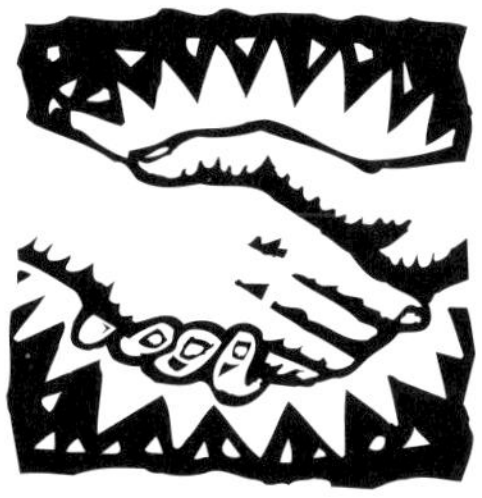

Name _____

Project _____

Due date _____

Materials/resources needed _____

_____

Plan for completing project _____

_____

_____

_____

Student signature _____ Teacher signature _____

Pick-a-Project Rubric

Name _____

	Project	Project	Project	Project	Project
The contracted number of projects has been completed.	1 2 3 4 5	1 2 3 4 5	1 2 3 4 5	1 2 3 4 5	1 2 3 4 5
Each project has been turned in on time.	1 2 3 4 5	1 2 3 4 5	1 2 3 4 5	1 2 3 4 5	1 2 3 4 5
Each project has been completed according to the directions on page 34.	1 2 3 4 5	1 2 3 4 5	1 2 3 4 5	1 2 3 4 5	1 2 3 4 5
Each project is neat and pleasant to read.	1 2 3 4 5	1 2 3 4 5	1 2 3 4 5	1 2 3 4 5	1 2 3 4 5
Each project is well organized and easy to understand.	1 2 3 4 5	1 2 3 4 5	1 2 3 4 5	1 2 3 4 5	1 2 3 4 5
Each project has been proofread for spelling and punctuation, and any errors have been neatly corrected.	1 2 3 4 5	1 2 3 4 5	1 2 3 4 5	1 2 3 4 5	1 2 3 4 5
Each project contains accurate information about New Mexico or the Southwest.	1 2 3 4 5	1 2 3 4 5	1 2 3 4 5	1 2 3 4 5	1 2 3 4 5
Each project is creative and fun.	1 2 3 4 5	1 2 3 4 5	1 2 3 4 5	1 2 3 4 5	1 2 3 4 5
Final score:					

PART 4:
MAPS
& RESOURCES

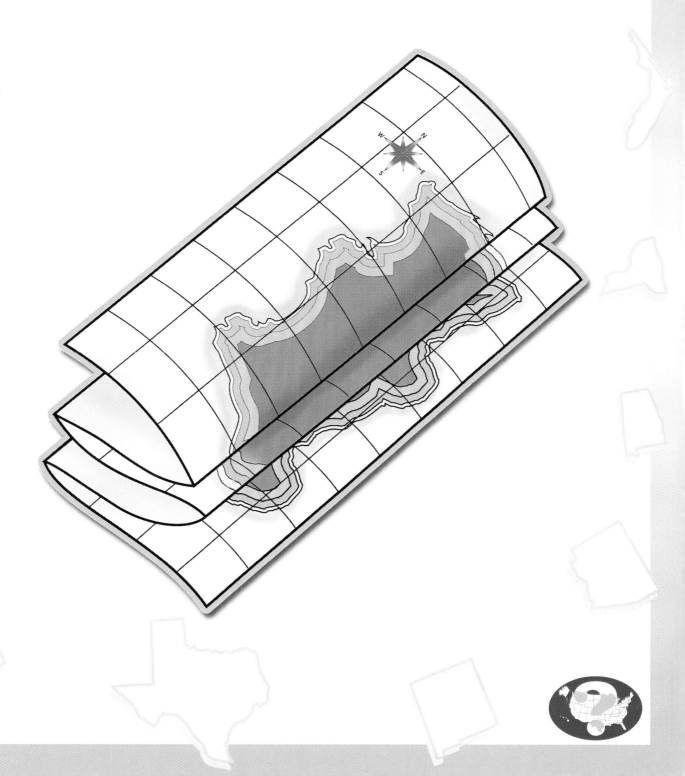

NEW MEXICO

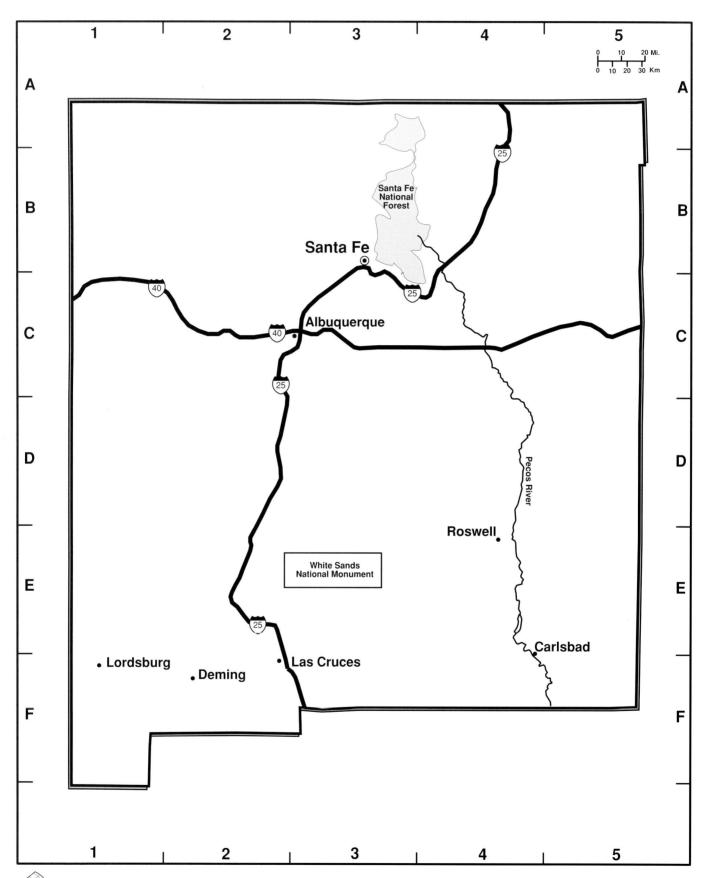

THE SOUTHWESTERN STATES

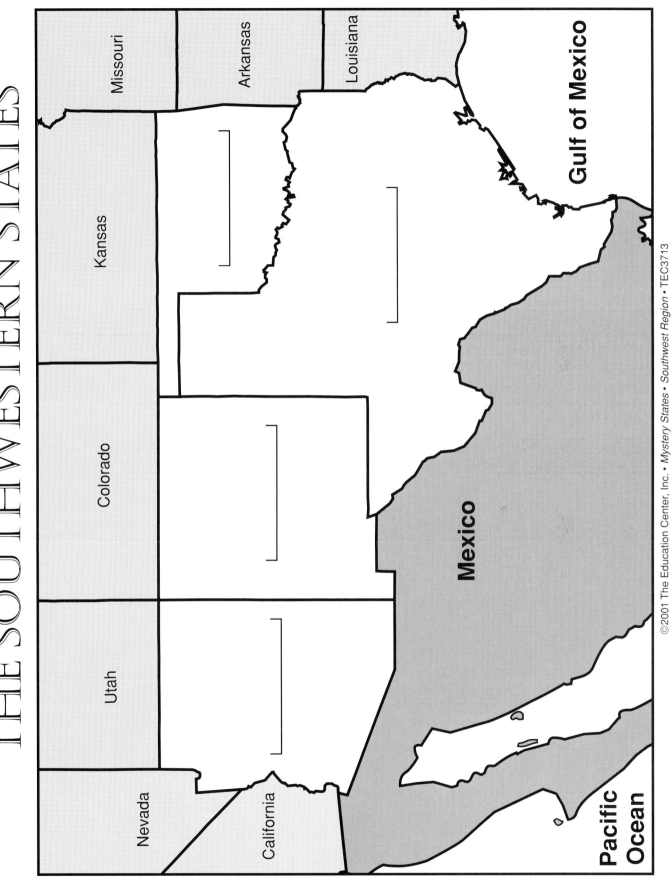

Missouri

Arkansas

Louisiana

Gulf of Mexico

Kansas

Colorado

Utah

Nevada

California

Mexico

Pacific Ocean

THE UNITED STATES

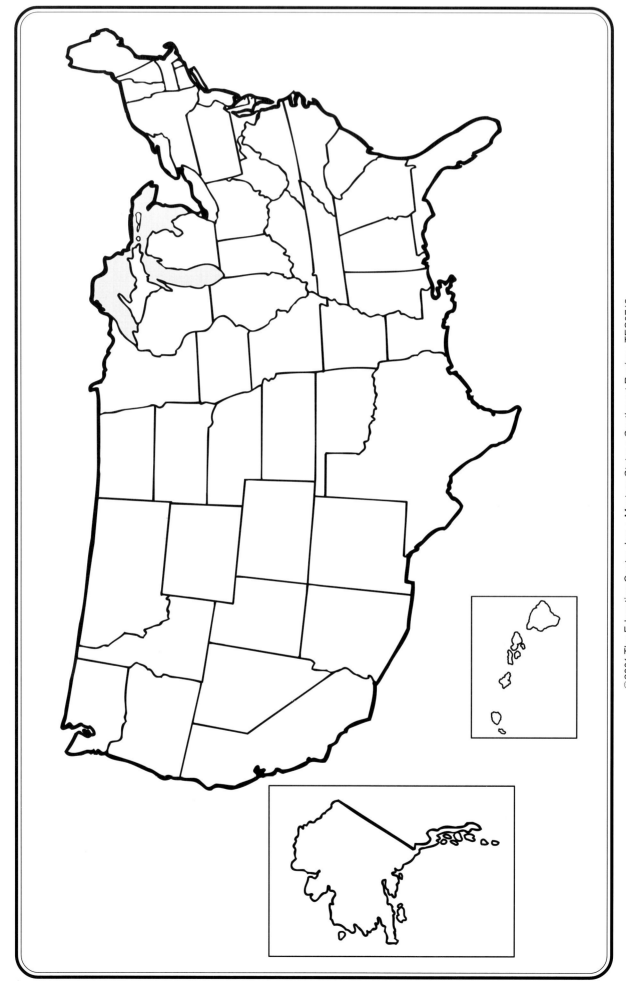

SYMBOLS OF NEW MEXICO

Resource Guide

Picture Books & Novels

And Now Miguel by Joseph Krumgold (HarperTrophy, 1984)

Big New Mexico Activity Book by Walter D. Yoder (Sunstone Press, 1997)

Carlos and the Squash Plant by Jan Romero Stevens (Rising Moon, 1995)

Curse of the Ruins (World of Adventure series) by Gary Paulsen (Bantam Books, Inc.; 1998)

The Day It Snowed Tortillas: Tales From Spanish New Mexico by Joe Hayes (Mariposa Printing and Publishing Company, 1985)

Dragonfly's Tale by Kristina Rodanas (Clarion Books, 1995)

Enchanted Runner by Kimberley Griffiths Little (Camelot, 1999)

The Farolitos of Christmas by Edward Gonzales (Hyperion Press Limited, 1995)

The Girl Who Chased Away Sorrow: The Diary of Sarah Nita, a Navajo Girl, New Mexico, 1864 by Ann Warren Turner (Scholastic Inc., 1999)

Little Juan Learns a Lesson by Joseph J. Ruiz (Sunstone Press, 1997)

Los Ojos del Tejedor: The Eyes of the Weaver by Cristina Ortega (Clear Light Publishers, 1997)

Meet Josefina, an American Girl (American Girls Collection series) by Valerie Tripp (Pleasant Company Publications, 1997)

My Land Sings: Stories From the Rio Grande by Rudolfo A. Anaya (Morrow Junior Books, 1999)

New Mexico A to Z by Dorothy Hines Weaver (Rising Moon, 1996)

New Mexico Facts and Symbols by Emily McAuliffe (Capstone Press, 1999)

Pueblo Boy: Growing Up in Two Worlds by Marcia Keegan (Clear Light Publishers, 2000)

Pueblo Storyteller by Diane Hoyt-Goldsmith (Holiday House, Inc.; 1994)

Rio Grande Stories by Carolyn Meyer (Gulliver Books, 1994)

Watch Out for Clever Women: Cuidado con las Muheres Astutas by Joe Hayes (Cinco Puntos Press, 1994)

Reference Books

Best of the Best From New Mexico Cookbook: Selected Recipes From New Mexico's Favorite Cookbooks by Gwen McKee (Quail Ridge Press, 1999)

Family Adventure Guide: New Mexico: Great Things to See and Do for the Entire Family by Catherine Coggan (Globe Pequot Press, 1996)

New Mexico (America the Beautiful, second series) by Deborah Kent (Children's Press, 1999)

New Mexico (From Sea to Shining Sea series) by Judith Bloom Fradin (Children's Press, 1994)

New Mexico (Hello U.S.A. series) by Theresa S. Early (First Avenue Editions, 1996)

New Mexico (One Nation series) by Patricia K. Kummer (Capstone Press, 1998)

New Mexico Rockhounding: A Guide to Minerals, Gemstones, and Fossils by Stephen M. Voynick (Mountain Press Publishing Company, 1997)

The Southwest: Colorado, New Mexico, Texas (Discovering America series) by Thomas G. and Virginia L. Aylesworth (Chelsea House Publishing, 1995)

Web Sites
(Current as of October 2000)

http://www.state.nm.us/state/FastFacts/funfacts.html— New Mexico Fast Facts site

http://www.newmexicom.com/—Online Guide to New Mexico

http://www.emnrd.state.nm.us/nmparks/—New Mexico State Park site

http://www.state.nm.us/—New Mexico State Government site

http://www.newmexico.org/—New Mexico Department of Tourism site

http://www.nps.gov/parks.html—National Parks Service site

http://www.nws.noaa.gov/—National Weather Service site

http://www.carlsbad.caverns.national-park.com— Carlsbad Caverns National Park site

Contacts

Carlsbad Caverns National Park
3225 National Parks Highway
Carlsbad, New Mexico 88220
(505) 785-2232

New Mexico State Parks Division
P.O. Box 1147
Santa Fe, NM 87504
1 (888) NMPARKS

Office of Statewide Programs & Education
Museum of New Mexico
P.O. Box 2087
Santa Fe, NM 87504-2087
(505) 476-5097

PART 5:
ANSWER KEYS
& CHECKLIST

Answer Keys

Page 16
Clue 1:
1. Arizona, California, Montana, Nevada, New Mexico, Oklahoma, Oregon, Utah, Wyoming
2. Arizona, New Mexico, Oklahoma

Clue 2:
1. Arizona, California, Colorado, Kansas, Montana, Nebraska, Nevada, New Mexico, North Dakota, Oklahoma, South Dakota, Texas, Utah, Wyoming
2. Arizona, New Mexico, Oklahoma, Texas

Clue 3:
1. Arizona, California, Colorado, Idaho, Nevada, New Mexico, Oregon, Texas, Utah, Wyoming
2. Arizona, New Mexico, Texas

Clue 4:
1. Arizona, Colorado, Idaho, Kansas, Montana, Nebraska, Nevada, New Mexico, North Dakota, Oklahoma, Oregon, South Dakota, Texas, Utah, Washington, Wyoming
2. Arizona, New Mexico, Oklahoma, Texas

Clue 5:
1. Arizona, California, Colorado, Nevada, New Mexico, Virginia
2. Arizona, New Mexico

Clue 6:
1. Arizona, California, Colorado, New Mexico, Oklahoma, Texas
2. Arizona, New Mexico, Oklahoma, Texas

Page 18
NEW MEXICO IS THE LAND OF ENCHANTMENT.

Page 20
State Capital: Santa Fe
State Tree: Piñon, or nut pine
State Flower: Yucca flower
State Bird: Roadrunner

(Answers will vary for the topics below. Possible answers are listed.)

Location
New Mexico is bordered on the north by Colorado, on the east by Oklahoma, on the east and south by Texas, on the west by Arizona, and on the northwest corner by Utah. Southern New Mexico borders Mexico.

Physical Land Features
New Mexico can be divided into four main land regions:
- Great Plains—eastern third of New Mexico, extend from a high northern plateau to the Pecos River Valley in the south, deep canyons in the plateau were cut by streams as the plateau sloped away from the Rocky Mountains
- Rocky Mountains—extend from Colorado into north-central New Mexico south toward Santa Fe, Wheeler Peak at 13,161 feet is the state's highest point
- Basin and Range Region—covers about a third of New Mexico, extends from the Rocky Mountains to Arizona and Mexico, includes scattered mountain ranges and desert basins
- Colorado Plateau—northwestern New Mexico; includes valleys, plains, canyons, cliffs, and *mesas* (flat-topped hills) such as Acoma

Natural Resources
Though more than half of New Mexico's soil isn't good for farming, it contains large mineral deposits. The state is rich in resources such as petroleum, natural gases, forests, grasses, plants, and animals.

Page 20 continued…
Climate & Weather
New Mexico's climate is warm and dry with plenty of sunshine and low humidity. Average July temperatures are 65°F in the north and 80°F in the south; 35°F in the north and 55°F in the south are the average January temperatures.

Page 21
Answers will vary. Possible answers include the following:

Native Americans
Native Americans have lived in New Mexico for at least 10,000 years. The Mogollon lived in valleys near the New Mexico–Arizona border. The Anasazi were a highly developed tribe who lived in the region where New Mexico, Arizona, Utah, and Colorado meet. Later tribes included the Navajo, Apache, Ute, and Comanche.

History
1540–1542—Francisco Vasquez de Coronado explored New Mexico in search of the Seven Cities of Cibola.
1598—The first permanent Spanish colony was founded at San Juan by Juan de Onate.
1609 or 1610—Santa Fe was established by Governor Pedro de Peralta.
1706—Albuquerque was founded by Francisco Cuervo y Valdes.
1848—New Mexico was ceded to the United States by Mexico.
1850—The Territory of New Mexico was created by Congress.
1912—On January 6, New Mexico became the 47th state.
1945—At Trinity Site, near Alamogordo, the first atomic bomb was exploded.

Famous Landmarks
Aztec Ruins National Monument—located north of Aztec, preserves the ruins of a 900-year-old Anasazi pueblo
Fort Union National Monument—located northeast of Las Vegas, New Mexico; preserves the ruins of an American fort that operated from 1851 to 1891 and is located along the Santa Fe Trail
Carlsbad Caverns National Park—located near Carlsbad, New Mexico; one of the world's biggest and most fascinating limestone caves
City of Rocks State Park—located northwest of Deming, interestingly shaped volcanic rock formations
Four Corners Monument—located near Farmington, the only spot in the United States where four states (New Mexico, Colorado, Arizona, and Utah) meet

Food
Beef—beef cattle are raised in nearly every part of the state
Chili peppers—one of the largest producers of chili peppers in the United States
Pecans—a top U.S. producer of pecans
Grain sorghum, onions, and wheat—also produced in New Mexico

Famous People
Judy Blume lives in Santa Fe. Blume has written several young adult novels.
William H. "Billy the Kid" Bonney was a well-known outlaw and cattle thief in the New Mexico Territory in the late 1800s.
Willa Sibert Cather was a resident of Santa Fe. She was an author and editor who won the Pulitzer Prize for fiction in 1923.
Geronimo was the leader of the Chiricahua Apache. He led surprise attacks in the New Mexico Territory and Mexico. He escaped a reservation but eventually surrendered in 1886.
Georgia O'Keeffe was a well-known painter who settled in New Mexico in 1949.
Robert Oppenheimer was the director of the Manhattan Project at Los Alamos, which developed the world's first atomic bomb from 1942 to 1945.

Answer Keys

Answers will vary. Possible answers include the following:

Economy

The *service industry* (community, business, and personal services; government; finance, insurance, and real estate; wholesale and retail trade; transportation, communication, and utilities) accounts for 69 percent of New Mexico's gross state product. *Manufacturing* (electrical equipment, chemicals, clothing, concrete, food products, petroleum products, primary metals, and printed materials) accounts for 17 percent of the gross state product. *Mining* (natural gas, petroleum, copper, and potash) accounts for 7 percent of the gross state product. *Agriculture* accounts for 2 percent of New Mexico's gross state product.

Plants

Trees found in New Mexico include aspens, cottonwoods, Douglas firs, junipers, piñons (nut pines), ponderosa pines, scrub oaks, spruces, and white firs.

Plants found in New Mexico include cacti, creosote bushes, gramma grasses, mesquite, white and purple sage, soapweed, and yucca flowers.

Animals

Animals found in New Mexico include badgers, beavers, black bears, bobcats, chipmunks, coyotes, deer, elk, foxes, jackrabbits, minks, mountain lions, otters, prairie dogs, and pronghorn.

Places of Interest

Tourist attractions in New Mexico include Carlsbad Caverns National Park, Los Alamos Bradbury Science Museum, San Miguel Mission, and any of New Mexico's 40 state parks.

Page 23

Albuquerque

1. The Albuquerque International Balloon Fiesta is the largest gathering of balloonists in the world.
2. The fiesta is held every year during the first weekend in October.
3. The fiesta lasts nine days. About 650 balloonists participate in the event.
4. Albuquerque is a great spot for the International Balloon Fiesta because it is surrounded by mountains and has unique weather and wind patterns called the "Albuquerque Box Effect." This allows balloonists to travel around the city in different directions and at different altitudes.

Hot-Air Balloons

1. The two main parts of a hot-air balloon are the *bag* and the *basket*. The bag inflates and lifts the basket. The basket holds the equipment, supplies, and passengers.
2. Hot-air balloons rise because the air inside the bag is heated by a propane burner. This heated air is warmer (and thus lighter) than the air surrounding it, making the balloon rise.
3. Most hot-air balloon flights take place early in the morning or late in the afternoon when winds are weaker.
4. Jean Francois Pilatre de Rozier, a French scientist, became the first person to fly a hot-air balloon on October 15, 1783.
5. The longest recorded hot-air balloon flight occurred in 1999 when Bertrand Piccard and Brian Jones circled the earth in 19 days, 1 hour, and 49 minutes and traveled approximately 25,402 miles.

Page 26

Judy Blume—Blume was born in 1938. She lives in Santa Fe, New Mexico. Blume has written several young adult novels.

Kit Carson—Carson helped organize New Mexican infantry volunteers during the American Civil War.

John Denver—Denver was born in Roswell, New Mexico, in 1943. He became a well-known singer after his hit album *Poems, Prayers, and Promises* was released in 1971.

Conrad Nicholson Hilton—Hilton was born in San Antonio, New Mexico, in 1887. In the 1960s, the Hilton Hotel System, which he founded, included more than 40 hotels in the United States and 40 hotels in countries all over the world.

Nancy Lopez—Lopez was raised in Roswell, New Mexico. Lopez was only 12 when she won the New Mexico Women's Amateur golf title. In her first year as a professional golfer, Lopez won nine tournaments.

Bill Mauldin—Mauldin was born in Mountain Park, New Mexico, in 1921. During World War II he drew cartoons of U.S. Army life for the armed forces newspaper *Stars and Stripes*. He went on to win the Pulitzer Prize for cartooning in 1945 and again in 1959.

Answer Keys

Page 27

Georgia O'Keeffe—O'Keeffe was born in 1887. She was a well-known painter. She admired the New Mexico landscapes and eventually moved to the state in 1949.

Harrison Schmitt—Schmitt was born in Santa Rita, New Mexico, in 1935. He is a geologist. Schmitt traveled aboard *Apollo 17* as the first scientist-astronaut in space. From 1977 to 1983 he represented New Mexico in the U.S. Senate.

Geronimo—Geronimo was born in 1829. He was the leader of the Chiricahua Apache. He led surprise attacks in the New Mexico Territory and in Mexico. He escaped from a reservation but eventually surrendered in 1886.

Billy the Kid—William Bonney is thought to have been born in 1859. He was a cattle thief and outlaw in the New Mexico Territory in the late 1800s.

Robert Oppenheimer—Oppenheimer was born in 1904. He was the director of the Manhattan Project at Los Alamos from 1942 to 1945. There he helped develop the world's first atomic bomb.

Willa Sibert Cather—Cather was born in 1873. She was a resident of Santa Fe. Cather received the 1923 Pulitzer Prize in fiction for her novel *One of Ours.*

Page 29

- False. Bats are not birds; they are mammals.
- True.   Bats are the only mammals that can fly.
- False. Bats are not blind. They can see probably as well as humans can.
- True.   There are 40 species of bats found in the United States.
- False. Bats don't attack people. They are timid creatures.
- True.   Most female bats only have one baby at a time.
- False. Of all the known bat species, only a few species of vampire bats feed on the blood of other animals. None of these bats live in the United States.
- False. Most bats live in crevices, burrows, buildings, or caves. Others live outside on trees or rocks.
- True.   Some bats navigate by making short, high-frequency sounds. Then they listen to the echoes to determine their location or how far they are from objects.
- False. Bats are good for the environment because they help control the insect population and pollinate plants.

Page 31

2. **Draw a star on the map to represent the location of each capital city. Then label each capital city on the map.**

   - <u>Phoenix</u> is the capital of Arizona.
   - <u>Santa Fe</u> is the capital of New Mexico.
   - <u>Austin</u> is the capital of Texas.
   - <u>Oklahoma City</u> is the capital of Oklahoma.

3. **Draw three brown triangles to represent the location of the mountain range below.**
   The <u>Rocky Mountains</u> stretch from northern New Mexico through western Texas.

4. **Label the map with a red box to show where each of the following desert or canyon areas are located.**
   - The <u>Grand Canyon</u> was formed by the Colorado River. It lies along the Colorado River between Lake Powell and Lake Mead.
   - The <u>Sonoran Desert</u> lies across southwest Arizona.

5. **Use a blue crayon or marker to color or trace each body of water on the map. Then label the body of water.**
   - The Rio Grande flows through the middle of <u>New Mexico</u>. It forms the border between <u>Texas</u> and Mexico.
   - The source of the Pecos River is in northern <u>New Mexico</u>. It flows through <u>New Mexico</u> and <u>Texas</u> and empties into the Rio Grande.
   - The Red River forms most of the border between <u>Oklahoma</u> and <u>Texas</u>.
   - The Colorado River flows through northwest <u>Arizona</u> and forms <u>Arizona's</u> western border.
   - Eufaula Lake is located in eastern <u>Oklahoma</u>.
   - Galveston Bay is located on the east coast of <u>Texas</u>.

46

Answer Keys

Page 32

Use the map below to check the appropriate parts of problems 1–6 on page 31.
(Map shows approximate locations.)

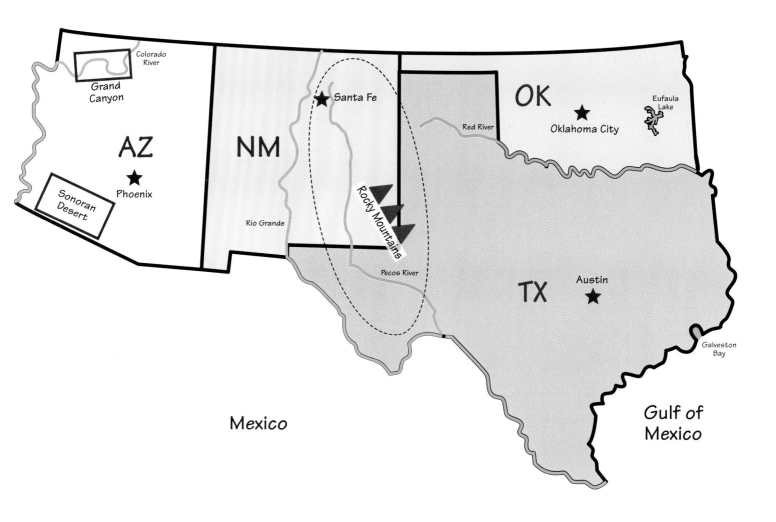

Activity
Checklist

Southwest	pp. 8–18	pp. 20–22	pp. 23–24	pp. 25–27	pp. 28–30	pp. 31–32	pp. 34–36		
Student Names	Solved the Mystery State	News About New Mexico	Balloons Over Albuquerque	Guess Who	Investigating Bats	Beyond the Borders of New Mexico	Pick-a-Project	Pick-a-Project Contract	Pick-a-Project Rubric